Stock Trading

Definitive Beginner's Guide

Table of Contents

Introduction 3

Chapter 1: Understanding Stocks 4

Chapter 2: Stock Market Basics 9

Chapter 3: Find the Right Mindset 14

Chapter 4: Getting Started 19

Chapter 5: Price Action Trading 25

Chapter 6: Trading Mistakes to Avoid 30

Chapter 7: Index Funds Versus Stocks 34

Chapter 8: Bears and Bulls 39

Conclusion 44

Introduction

Congratulations on purchasing *Stock Trading: Definitive Beginner's Guide* and thank you for doing so. When it comes to making a real change to your financial future there are few better ways of going about doing so than by investing in the stock market.

Unfortunately, the road to a profitable trading strategy is fraught with peril which is why the following chapters will explain everything you ever wanted to know about stocks, how to get in the right mindset to trade stocks effectively, how to go about actually making your first trade, how to find prospective trades using price action trading and elucidating many of the most common mistakes new traders make so you can more easily avoid them. Finally, you will also learn the differences between stocks and index funds as well as the key differences between a bull market and a bear market and how to take advantage of both for maximum profit.

There are plenty of books on this subject on the market, thanks again for choosing this one! Every effort was made to ensure it is full of as much useful information as possible, please enjoy!

Chapter 1:
Understanding Stocks

When it comes to building wealth, there are few more well-known, or effective ways of doing so than effectively playing the stock market. As such, they are part of any quality investment portfolio which is why you are going to want to learn just what they are all about as soon as possible. This is especially true because stock market trading is becoming a more and more common way for not just the wealthy few, but anyone with an internet connection to make money in a number of different ways.

Companies issue stock for one reason and one reason only, as a way to raise capital. Issuing a first round of stock is a company's ownership deciding to cede a portion of the control of their company to outsiders as a way of raising capital for future growth. Issuing stock is what is known as equity financing. While the company is giving up a specific share of ownership in the company, in return they gain access to a source of revenue that they do not need to worry about paying back. Initial shareholders who buy into unproven companies are taking a risk that the stock will be worth more than what they are buying in for in return for potential big rewards if the initial stock evaluation is especially favorable. The first time that a company decides to sell a portion of its stock is referred to as an initial public offering.

Unfortunately, many people still have an antiquated view of the stock market that was primarily codified in the late 1990s during the dotcom boom. During this period, the introduction of the internet not only let more people interact with the stock market than ever before, it also meant that the number of online businesses going public for the first time ended up making a widely publicized handful of individuals extremely rich. It doesn't matter that the dotcom boom was followed by major dotcom fallout, this high risk and high reward mentality has permeated many people's view of the stock market ever since. The reality, of course is that the amount of risk to take when investing in the stock market is going to be different for everyone. Therefore, it is important to know as much about it up front as possible.

What is a stock exactly?

At its most basic, one share of stock is a representation of a partial claim to a given company's earnings and assets. The more shares of a company's stock that are available overall, the less each individual share is worth. The more shares of a company you own, the more control you have over the company in question. Stock can also be referred to as equity or shares as well. Those who own stock in a company are referred to as that company's shareholders which means they each get a share of profits, known as dividends, at predetermined periods throughout the year and also, in some cases, voting rights based on the number of shares in a company that they hold.

While originally each stock that you owned came with a physical piece of paper indicating what you owned as well as how much, these days all of this information is stored electronically by the brokerage that you will ultimately choose to directly handle your transactions. While holding a physical copy of your shares is nice, it would also require you to take those documents to the brokerage you were using every time you wanted to make a trade. This process is referred to as the in street name method of holding shares.

While owning shares of a company does entitle you to a piece of their profits, it does not mean that you can have an active say in how the business is run, even if you own voting shares. At most, you are going to be able to vote for board of director members at an annual shareholders' meeting. During this meeting you will be able to cast your vote and it will be weighted based on the number of shares of the company's stock that you hold. The goal of this process is to provide shareholders a way of indicating their pleasure or displeasure with the overall way the company is being run. Unless you own a significant portion of the overall number of shares of a company you really won't have much say in what they do.

Be aware of the risk

When it comes to investing in the stock market, it is important to keep in mind which of the companies you invest in actually pay out dividends. Companies are not obligated to process dividends, even if that is traditionally how things have been done in the past. As such, the only type of profit that you can be sure to count on is the value made through appreciation, assuming the stock performs positively. There are dozens of reasons that a given stock can suddenly start to slip, or for the underlying company to go completely bankrupt, potentially even with little or no notice.

While risk can generally be often thought of as a negative, it should instead be considered a tool because the greater the amount of risk that any given stock presents, the greater amount of reward it will naturally contain as well. Understanding what the right amount of risk is for you- which we will discuss in detail in chapter 4- is crucial to getting the best possible return from your investment. So much so, that smart stock market investment routinely out performs the standard 7 percent return that most investments provide. All told, you can generally expect a 10 percent return when investing in stocks, with as much as 12 percent being possible as well.

Just because you aren't going to have a say in the company in question, doesn't mean that you won't get to share in the rewards which is why a majority of those who invest in stocks do so in a passive way. Alternatively, you can trade stocks instead of investing in them and make it an active income stream instead. As a shareholder you are entitled to profit dividends as well as a share of the company's assets if it ends up in bankruptcy. In addition to a share of the profits, stock ownership is what is known as limited liability which means you will not be liable for any debts that the company is otherwise unable to pay.

Types and classes of stock

Common stock: Stock can generally be broken down into one of two main types. Common stock is, as the name implies is the more common of the two. In fact, when stocks are being discussed, the odds are good that this is the type of stock that people are talking about. Common stock is the type of stock that the previous section discussed in detail, and it entitles the owner to a partial ownership of a company and a portion of any related dividends. Common stock is known to carry more risk, as well as more potential for reward than other investments.

Preferred stock: On the other hand, preferred stock gives an individual right to a small portion of the ownership of a company, though without any of the related voting rights that come with shares of common stock. Additionally, preferred stock entitles the owner to a set rate of dividends in perpetuity, as long as the related company remains in business. This guarantee is what makes this stock preferred as common stock carries no guarantees of any types. Additionally, if you own shares of preferred stock then you know that you will be paid out before common stock holding shareholders if the related company goes out of business. However, if you own preferred stock then the related company also has the right to buy back the stock for a premium price at any time without your consent.

Class A stock or Class B stock: While there are two main types of stock, there are also multiple different classes of stock that companies can delegate if they only want a certain group of investors to retain voting power. Of the two, Class A stock is generally considered to be the group that retains voting rights, while those same rights are not extended to Class B.

Chapter 2:
Stock Market Basics

Every stock is traded on what is known as an exchange, or market, with the most well-known of these likely being the New York Stock Exchange (NYSE). While exchanges used to be limited to purely physical locations, many are now primarily online with a system of computers making all of the trades required in real time. The stock market exists as a way to make securities exchanges as simple and easy as possible, while at the same time cutting down on the potential for risk as well. Each stock market can then be broken down into two parts, the primary market as well as the secondary market. The primary market consists of newly created stocks that have come into being because new companies have had their initial public offering. Meanwhile the secondary market is the market with which most people are already familiar where existing stock are traded on a daily basis.

Trading in the major markets

US: There are two primary markets in the United States, the NYSE and the Nasdaq. In the NYSE the trading is still done face to face while on an actual trading floor. It is what is known as a listed exchange which means that orders to sell and orders to buy are constantly coming through all day, as long as the market is open. Orders are then matched between potential buyers and sellers with prices being determined by the most and least that any buyer is will to pay for the share in question. Almost all of the biggest companies in the US are currently listed on the NYSE.

While the NYSE is still based on physical trading that happens on the trading floor, the other major exchange in the US, the Nasdaq is an over the counter virtual market. As the name implies, this means that the Nasdaq has no central location and is instead comprised entirely of electronic communications. While many of the largest companies in the country are housed on the NYSE, the Nasdaq is home to many of the biggest technology companies in the country including the likes of Intel, Cisco and Microsoft. When working with Nasdaq, brokerages then play the role of market maker when it comes to the stocks in question. A market maker is someone whose job it is to generate a steady stream of offers to buy (called bids) and sell (called asks) within a set range (called the spread) for a set stock or groups of stocks. While these brokers may also match up individual interested buyers with motivated sellers, they will also keep a portion of shares to ensure investors can be satisfied at all times.

Other Choices: While the NYSE and Nasdaq are two of the largest stock markets in the world, they are still only a small part based on the total of what is available. Virtually every country in the world has their own stock exchange, but the other major hubs of note are in England with the London Stock Exchange and in Hong Kong with the Hong Kong Stock Exchange. Finally, what is known as the over the counter bulletin board is an online exchange that primarily deals in smaller unregulated companies. The stocks related to these types of business and are referred to as penny stocks and are typically considered extremely risky and not worth the hassle for those new to investing in the stock market.

Market forces

While there are numerous different reasons that could cause the price of a given stock to vary dramatically, the majority of change that most stocks see in a day is caused by basic supply and demand. If a particular company reports on good news then this will make more people want to buy its stock, thus increasing its demand. Likewise, if the amount of a company's stock that is currently available is greater than the demand then the excessive supply is going to cause the price to decrease instead. Despite the fact that these concepts are extremely easy to grasp, the reasons for why either supply or demand move in a given direction can be extremely complicated.

As previously touched on, when a company receives good news their stock price typically increases, unfortunately interpreting news can be difficult in and of itself. Additionally, you are going to want to keep the principal theory in mind as well, specifically, you do not want to make the mistake of equating the current price of a stock with what that company is worth. Instead, the value of a company must be determined through a process known as market capitalization whereby the current price of the stock is factored into the total number of available shares. As an example, if a given company has a share value of $50, as well as 5 million total shares in the market, then you can safely assume that company is worth 250 million dollars.

Companies are also evaluated based on the expectations that investors have for them as well as on their earnings. Earnings are the sum total of what a company made in a given quarter after all expenses have been calculated. Public companies (those that have stock traded on the market) must report their earnings every three months, with each quarter being referred to as an individual earning season. These reports are then used by analysts to determine an estimate of what the next quarter should also look like. If the results don't match the previous expectations, then the price of the related stock is going to drop and if they exceed expectations the price is going to rise.

Finally, the most difficult variable to pin down ahead of time is public opinion. The history of the stock market is full of examples of companies that experienced extremely high stock prices for a prolonged period of time despite never actually generating any earnings. While investing in stocks that are on the rise when it comes to public opinion can be extremely profitable, putting public opinion ahead of financial statements is always a risky move because you never known when market opinion is going to shift back in the other direction.

P/E ratio: As such, whenever you come across a stock that is currently experiencing a high degree of popularity then determining its share price and it earnings per share, known as the P/E ratio. To determine this ratio, you are going to want to start by taking the current value of a share and dividing that by the amount of earnings the company last reported broken down into a per share price. As an example, if a company had a current share price of $43 as well as $1.95 worth of earnings per share then to find the P/E ratio you would simply divide 43 by 1.95 to get a P/E ratio of 22.05.

The price to earnings ratio can be thought of as how much you would need to invest in a given company in order to see $1 of return in the form of the company in question's earnings. In the above example, investors appear to currently be willing to pay just over $22 in order to see $1 of company profit. As a general rule of thumb, the higher the P/E ratio is, the greater the overall level of performance that investors expect from the stock in question. When you find a company with a low P/E ratio then the company is possibly undervalued currently, especially if it has recently been posting record profits. You will not see negative P/E ratios discussed, though they can be calculated, instead, companies that are not currently turning a profit have their P/E ratio listed as not applicable.

A P/E ratio does have a number of limitations, however, which will need to be factored in if you hope to use the results with any accuracy. First and foremost, the P/E ratios of various different industries are typically going to vary dramatically. This means that a P/E ratio cannot be accurately thought of as a comparison tool outside of the business sector in question. Additionally, a P/E ratio does not accurately factor in the risk/reward related to taking on additional debt which will lead to inaccurate results in some cases. Finally, it is important to keep in mind that many publicly traded companies use complicated accounting techniques to obfuscate the true results of their most recent quarter which can lead to false results as well.

Chapter 3:
Find the Right Mindset

While you will often find individuals who use the terms investing in stocks and trading stock interchangeably, in reality the two are different in several distinct ways. As such, the first step to getting into the right mindset to deal with the stock market is to understand the differences between the two. For starters, the basic difference is that if you are investing you are going to be looking to find stocks that are going to pay off in the long term which generally means six months or more from when you purchased them. If, on the other hand, you are holding onto stocks for a day or two, at the most, then you are trading stocks instead of investing in them.

If you plan on trading stocks, then this means you are going to want to working the market every single day in order to ensure that you turn a profit. If you choose to proceed down this path, it is important to know that it is a very fluid process and your investment funds will likely be bouncing between a number of different companies throughout a day as opposed to being left unattended for months at a time in hopes of scoring a long term profit. If you are unsure if you have a mindset that is suited to one or another, the first thing you are going to want to determine is how much time you plan on spending actively engaged in researching the market as well as how long you plan to spend actively engaged in making trades. Being an investor means spending chunks of time doing research whenever you are interested in adding to your portfolio. Being a trader means spending a significant portion of every day doing research on the current state of the market and doing everything you can to keep up with the competition all before the market even opens and the real trading begins.

Finally, when it comes to investing you can expect about 5 percent return on your investment per year, for very little work, while trading can result in up to a 12 percent return but should be more accurately thought of as a full time job rather than a passive income stream. If you still aren't sure which direction is the best for you, then if you are interested in buying stock in a particular company, the type of investment that company turns out to be could make the decision for you. If you are interested in working with a company that is going to produce reliable year-over-year results then you are going to be investing, if the company is known for high highs and low lows, then trading is a better choice.

The trading mindset

Chapter 4 concerns itself with making a plan when it comes to playing the stock market and the specifics involved in your first trade. Making a plan is useless, however, if you don't have the proper mindset going into the experience to maximize its effectiveness as much as possible. To that end, it is important that you keep the following tips in mind for the best results.

- *Always remain flexible:* The stock market is always fluctuating which means that if you are ever going to be successful, you are going to need to be just as flexible. The market can change in a moment and valuable stocks can end up being worthless in the blink of an eye. To succeed you must stop thinking about the past and instead exclusively focus on the present and the future. You need to be ready to ditch trades that are turning on you and reevaluate those you previously passed on at a moment's notice if you hope to have the best results possible.

- *Commit to your plan:* The plan you create will be critical to your success in the stock market, but only if you follow it to the letter every single time you put it into action. Knowing what criteria are acceptable when it comes to both buying and selling at any given time is crucial to being able to take advantage of emerging trends in the moment.

- *Don't expect too much too soon:* As previously noted, the stock market is rarely a place where fortunes are lost in a single stroke. This means that you are going to either need to commit to a few stocks for the long term or commit to the act of trading regularly if you hope to see any real results. Additionally, you will want to keep in mind a realistic timetable for when those profits are going to start to appear as many people require multiple months of trial and error before they can consistently make money from trades on a reliable basis. Going into the process with a realistic idea of what it's going to take to be successful is a great way to make the learning curve more manageable.

- *Find the right strategies that work for you:* Just because you hear of a strategy that works for someone else is no guarantee that this same strategy will work for you. While there is no reason not to try out a presumably proven system for yourself, it is important to ensure that it lines up with your natural inclinations as well otherwise, no matter how effective someone else found it to be, you will find that you are working twice as hard for half the results. Always be on the lookout for plans that use your natural inclinations as stepping stones to success, not barriers that need to be circumvented each and every time. Remain true to yourself and you will see better results every time, practically guaranteed.

Focus on discipline

Many new traders find themselves going after specific stocks or types of stocks simply because they have a gut feeling. Unfortunately, very few people can effectively trust their gut when it comes to trading stocks which means this scattershot policy will not only make it more difficult for you make a profit overall, but it can teach you bad habits along the way as well. As such, rather than focusing on what your gut is telling you, a better choice is to instead work on building your trading discipline by following the rules outlined below with every single trade you make. It might be hard to go against your gut at first, but over time you will be glad you did.

- *Look for an absolute truth:* It doesn't matter if you feel that a specific price for a given stock is too high or too low, the only thing you can reliably focus on in the moment is the price as it currently stands. If the facts say that a stock should be valued higher, you buy, if it says lower you sell, end of story. It is important to remain impartial about every stock you purchase as forming an attachment is the surest way to lose objectivity.

- *Be logical:* Once you have formed a successful plan, following it to the letter every time is always going to be the logical choice. As such, if you follow your plan to the letter and a trade doesn't work out in the way that you expect there is no reason angry with yourself as you still made the proper choice. As long as your plan returns positive results more than 50 percent of the time you are going to make a profit, keep this in mind and you will see the failed trades for what they are, the statistical balance to the rest of your success.

- *Don't be afraid to do nothing:* If signs point to a particular stock currently being undervalued then the right choice is to buy, just as when a stock appears overvalued the right choice is to sell. As such, if indicators say that a particular stock is not going to move much at all during a given period the right choice is to way for things to change. Many new traders find themselves with a mindset that prioritizes daily action of any sort over a well-considered pause. This is often folly, however, as if the market isn't moving much at all, or it is in too much of a state of flux to read accurately then the right answer is very much to wait and see when you can make trades in your favor. Remember, the end goal is to make profitable trades, not just to make trades for the sake of trading.

- *Don't waste time looking for surefire methods:* The odds of finding a system that can accurately predict trades of 100 percent, or even close to 100 percent are, statistically speaking, less likely than of you winning the lottery. There are simply too many variables to consider at all times, and there is no way of accounting for chance to boot. Instead of wasting time on pie in the sky dreams, a better choice is to instead look for a generally reliable plan instead.

Chapter 4:
Getting Started

When it comes time to prepare to make your first trade, you are going to need to choose the way you are going to purchase stocks that is right for you, understand how to read a stock quote accurately and finalize your trading plan. Only by ensuring that all three are in order will you know that you are getting started with the greatest overall chance of success possible.

Purchase Stocks

The primary way that many traders and investors interact with stocks is via a brokerage. A brokerage brokers deals between interested sellers and interested buyers, all the while charging a fee for each trade that is made as well as a commission. Furthermore, there are two primary types of brokerages these days, those that offer a variety of services including trading advice or those that offer an online, more barebones approach. Full service brick and mortar brokerages frequently have a historical record of trade success that you can look into, though they are almost always going to cost you more than if you went with an online brokerage instead.

When you are looking into various brokerages you may find that it is difficult to compare them accurately as many can spin the same similarities and differences in various ways. Regardless, it is important to persevere as finding the right brokerage for you could very well be the difference between overall success and failure of your stock market plans. You will want to persevere and determine the various differences in fee structures and services that various brokerages are offering so that you will be in the best position possible to take full advantage of what is being offered to you. You are always going to want to determine what their margin rates are like, what their commissions are like, what people online are saying about their trading platform, what the account minimum is going to be and what promotions they are currently running.

Alternatively, you can choose to investment in stocks via a dividend reinvestment plan or a direct investment plan. Referred to as DRIPs and Dips respectively, these types of plans allow shareholders to buy stock related to a specific company directly for the company in question. Specifically, in order for this type of transaction to occur you would need to already own shares of a company in question that is paying dividends, you will then sometimes have the opportunity to reinvest those dividends in additional shares of the company.

Reading a stock quote

Regardless of the broker and platform you ultimately choose, when you log into it and chose a stock to look at in detail you are going to be greeted with up to 12 columns of relevant information.

Column 1: The first column you are going to see is going to be the highest price the stock in question has hit in the past year, not including the most previous day in most cases.

Column 2: The second column is going to be the opposite of column 1, that is, it is going to show the lowest amount the stock in question has traded at in the last year, not including the previous day.

Column 3: The third column is home to the name of the company, generally abbreviated, as well as the type of stock that is being traded. If all you see in this column is the name of the company in question, then the related stock is always going to be common. If the stock is instead preferred, then it will be noted with a "pf" after the name.

Colum 4: The fourth column is going to contain the ticker symbol for the company in question. The ticker is the symbol that is shown in stock price overviews when it comes to determining price in an up to the minute fashion.

Column 5: The fifth column shows what the annual dividend for the company in question is going to be, written in the form of payment per share. If this column holds no information, then the company won't be paying dividends.

Column 6: The sixth column holds the information related to the percentage of a return that the information in column 5 actually provides.

Column 7: The seventh column shows the P/E ratio discussed in chapter 2.

Column 8: The eighth column lists the number of shares of the stock in question that have been traded during the current day so far. The amount is written as hundreds which means all you need to do is add a pair of zeroes to the end of the written number to get the true number.

Column 9: The ninth column will show you the current range the stock in question is trading at so far for the day, specifically the highest price for the day.

Column 10: The tenth column will show you the current range the stock in question is trading at so far for the day, specifically the lowest price for the day.

Column 11: If the market has closed for the day then the eleventh column will tell you the last price that the stock in question traded at. If the stock in question has moved at least 5 percent in either direction, then the entire listing is going to be in bold.

Column 12: The final column will show you how much value has changed in the stock in question compared to where it was at 24 hours before. The more positive net change you can find, the better.

Prepare your plan

When you are actually ready to start putting your own personal trading plan together, the first thing you will want to do is to determine what sector of stocks you are going to want to focus on, a specific sector will make research much easier, as well as how much you have to start investing with and if you are looking for short term or long term investments. Finally, you are going to want to determine how much time you have to devote to trading each week and what type of return on your investment you are looking for.

With this information in mind, you can then determine how much risk you are going to be required to take in order to see the type of results you are looking for. If you don't like the results you can either change the amount you hope to make in return, the amount of risk you are willing to take or the amount you are starting with, the overall result is always going to be a balance of these three. This doesn't mean that you should be setting daily trading goals, however, as doing so is only going to lead to poor trading habits and greater losses in the long run.

With these details in mind, and through the use of a strategy chosen from the next three chapters you can then determine what type of signals you are going to be looking for when it comes to getting into, or out of various trades. In order to ensure that you don't lose more than is necessary if a trade turns sour, you are going to want to ensure that you always set what are known as stop losses, with every trade you make. A stop loss is the automated point at which you sell off your shares to prevent additional losses. The closer a stop loss is to the amount you entered into a trade in, the less likely you are to lose out on a risky investment.

Additionally, you will always want to determine a point that you are going to walk away from the trade in question when you have made enough profit to satisfy your requirements. Instead of striving to squeeze every penny out of each profitable trade, it is important to set an exit point that takes a majority of the profits while increasing the risk as minimally as possible. Furthermore, if you just don't want to part with a particular stock, you can instead sell off half of your holdings and set a new higher exit point to split the risk and reward difference.

When it comes to determining whether or not your plan is actually successful, you are going to want to analyze your results after at least a week, never only a day or two as the limited data can easily skew things in an unprofitable direction. Instead, you are going to want to keep detailed notes regarding when trades were made, what indicators were considered, the costs incurred and if it ended in success or failure. Remember, as long as your plan has a successful trade percentage of greater than 50 percent then you are likely to make an overall profit in the long run.

Finally, and perhaps most importantly, once you have a successful trading plan in mind, it is important to stick with it as thoroughly as possible, even when your emotions are urging you to act in a different fashion than what your plan would recommend. When trading, your goal should be to reduce the input that your emotions have on the process as completely as possible. Trading successfully is all about the numbers, and emotions are only going to get in the way. The more robotically you can trade on the regular, the greater your profits are going to be in both the short and the long term. If you ever find yourself preparing to make a trade based on emotion, simply ask yourself if you would have made this same trade if your emotions weren't in play and you will find an actionable answer.

Chapter 5:
Price Action Trading

While many active traders make use of complicated indicators that have to do with reading charts and drawing figures based on complex formulas, as a new trader you are likely going to be much better served by starting with price action trading instead. While some new traders may turn their noses up at anything that professional traders aren't currently using, the reality is that indicator based trading only works for the experts because they have already learned how to compensate for its flaws. As such, if you are brand new to the process then you are going to want to start with something that can be understood easily and work on improving your trade percentage before you need to start worrying about finding more complicated ways to pick the stocks that you ultimately do trade.

At its most basic, price action can be thought of as a way for a trader to determine the current state of the market based on the way that prices are currently acting as opposed to what one of dozens of different indicators has to say about it after the fact. As such, if you are a trader that is interested in getting started as quickly as possible then sticking with price action trading for now can save you serous time as you only have to spend your time and focus studying the market as it is in the present. Additionally, focusing exclusively on the price and the price alone will help you to avoid much of the unnecessary information that is constantly circling the market, blocking out the static and increasing your overall chance of success.

Getting started with price action trading

To get started using price action to determine when to trade, all you are going to need is the basics that come with the brokerage and trading platform you have chosen, starting with price bars. A price bar is simply a representation of relevant price information for a set period of time, typically in units of 5 minutes, 30 minutes, 1 hour, daily or weekly. In order to create an accurate price bar, you need four different pieces of information, the first the is the amount the stock in question opened at, the second is the overall high for the day, the third is the overall low for the day and the fourth is the price it closed at. From there, the data is plotted in such a way that it looks like a box with a line through it. The two end points of the line represent the high and low respectively when the top and bottom edges of the box represent the opening and closing prices respectively. Stocks that ended on an appreciation profit are one color and those that suffered a loss are a second color.

The result can also be referred to as a candlestick and in addition to summarizing a day's worth of information, it provides new information that is crucial for make the right price action trade decision when the time is right, this includes the range of the stock, the body of the stock and the upper wick and lower wick.

Range: The range is a visual representation of the market's current level of volatility. The bigger the box is in relation to the line, also known as the wick, the more active the market currently is and the higher the overall degree of volatility. The greater the amount of volatility the market is currently experiencing the higher the amount of risk you take on by making a move.

Body: Body refers to the physical orientation of the box in question, this means that if the close is above the open then the market improved and if it the price closes underneath the open then the market decreased in value. What's more, when looking at the box you are going to want to take note of how large the box is in relation to the wick. The larger the box is in relation to the wick, the stronger the market is overall. If there is absolutely no bar to speak of then the market is said to be undecided. If you come across traders talking about marubozu, this is a candle with no wick and doji is a market that is still undecided.

Top wick/bottom wick: After you have a clear idea of the body as well as the range of a candle, you are then able to accurately determine what the upper wick is telling you. The upper wick shows the uppermost point that the price reached in a given time frame that was unable to be matched by overall market movement. What this wick signifies is that after the price rose to the top point the number of sellers was greater than the number of buyers so the price dropped again instead of rising. As such, the top wick can be thought of as the amount of pressure to sell that the stock in question experienced in the given time frame. Likewise, the lower wick indicates how strong the pressure to buy was on the stock in question. The longer either wick remains, the greater the overall strength of the pressure in question.

Adding a second price bar

If you add a second price bar to your analysis you will find that you now have a pair of cornerstones to determine price, testing as well as context. Essentially what the second bar provides is a way to determine if the data from the first bar is actually relevant or merely an outlier of no statistical significance.

Specifically, it is useful when it comes to things like determining if a bar that is wide is actually wide or simply on par with other bars for the time period in question. This, in turn, allows you to describe the price action in a more specific way. Additionally, having a second bar will allow you to determine if a given price level will be enough to break through either the support or the resistance. If the second bar shows the same levels of support or resistance, then it is unlikely that the price action is going to break through it. Likewise, if the two candles have difference levels of support or resistance, then it is more likely that a breakthrough can be made.

Adding a third price bar

Adding in a third bar allows you to confirm the hypothesis that adding in a second bar allowed you to determine. The third bar should then be shown to move in such a way that it soundly confirms or denies what your expectations of the market were up until this point. The idea here is that if a market is strong it will continue to be so, and the same goes for when it is weak as well. If the market lacks inertia, then it is possible for a change to come about at any time. It is important to keep in mind that even with three bars the results are going to remain quite short term and taking this pattern to be anything other than a short term one is likely to be folly without significant follow up.

What it all means

What this type of strategy provides you with is a clear idea of what support and resistance levels are like for the time period in question which, in turn, allows you to pick trades with a higher degree of certainty. All you need to remember is that if demand is going to be stronger than the supply the price is going to increase. If you are aware that this is likely what is going to happen in the future, then all you have to do is estimate the point at which it is likely to happen and suddenly you have a point that you will want to enter on. Likewise, if you notice that supply is suddenly starting to outpace demand, then you are going to want to sell as quickly as possible in order to avoid losing out on profits that you have already made. Remember, when a price reaches the support level then you can realistically expect demand to exceed supply and if it reaches the resistance level then you can expect supply to exceed demand instead. Keep this in mind and trade accordingly.

Chapter 6:
Trading Mistakes to Avoid

If you are planning to start trading stocks instead of merely investing in them, then you are likely going to be dealing with a wider variety of stocks as you move through different positions quickly throughout the day. All this back and forth means that regularly making a few different mistakes can be enough to wipe out your initial investment amount and kill your trading career before it even gets off the ground. Avoid the following common mistakes and you just might make it long enough to stop being considered a novice.

Never let losses build: If you ever hope to be a truly successful trader then you are going to need to learn how to keep your expectations for a trade separate from reality. A successful trader knows that as soon a trade enters loss territory it is rarely going to rebound enough that it actually makes a decent profit and as such, they find that it is best to nip losses in the bud as early as possible. New traders often make the mistake of sticking with certain trades, even after signs begin pointing to a loss because they take trading personally, possibly because they think a failed trade is a reflection on them, or because they simply don't like to lose. Regardless of the reasons behind it, doubling down on a losing trade is only ever asking for trouble.

Like simply sticking with a losing trading, many new traders are also fond of buying in at an additional amount for a losing trade in yet another effort to turn things around. While this type of strategy can work for those who are investing, trying this while trading is akin to flushing your money down the drain. Adding to a losing position is like trying to dig yourself out of a hole, it is never going to work no matter how hard you try.

This is why it is so important to get comfortable setting stop losses that align with the level of risk that you are willing to take with the stock you are currently trading. While it is always possible that a stop loss could trigger due to the natural ebb and flow of price, the simple fact that they are guaranteed to prevent you from dealing with staggering losses is enough to make them worth the risk. Many new traders go to the trouble of setting a decent stop loss only to cancel it right before it is about to trigger in hopes that things are going to turn around. Treat stop losses as part of your plan and never alter your plan when your emotions are control your actions, doing so is only asking for trouble.

Never trade just to trade: It often takes new traders a while to properly calibrate their trading compasses when it comes to quantity versus quality. As such, it can be easy to get yourself to a position where it seems that if you are not making trades constantly, then you are doing something wrong. It is important to keep in mind, however, that contrary to how it might first appear, trading too often can actually cut into your profit margins quite significantly. Most plans calculate their success based on well thought out and research trades. If you are getting itchy about not trading enough then you likely aren't going to be making well thought out trades, you are likely going to be mean doing what your emotions tell you which is, at best, a risky proposition. Extra trades mean extra chances for loss, while poorly researched trades mean extra chances for loss as well. With these type of odds is it any wonder why these types of trades can quickly destroy all your profits?

Going with the flow: As a new trader, it can be easy to get swept up in the moment when you find a stock that it seems absolutely everyone is jumping on and rush to do so as well. While trading with the trend is typically a good idea, it is always a better idea to jump in on that trend as early as possible so that you can make the most of it in as many ways as possible. This means you need to be aware of not only the right time to jump into a trade, but also the point at which profit has been maximized and staying has the potential to hurt you more than it could help you. Unfortunately, the variables involved in determining such things are so varied that the only way to learn which is which is through practice. Don't forget, sometimes going against the majority is the best way to make a profit.

Always do your research before jumping into the market: As a new trader, it can be easy to reach a point where you are tired of learning about the stock market and are anxious to start working with it in earnest instead. This is a dangerous proposition, however, as starting to make trades before you are truly ready is an easy way to erode any profits you do make extremely quickly. Especially early on, you need to constantly be learning everything you can in order to ensure you can point out things like seasonal trends, trends based on newly released information as well as trading patterns in general. If you absolutely, positively, can't wait one more moment to trade you are free to give into your impulses, just be prepared for the possibility of learning an expensive lesson for the privilege.

Taking on too much too soon: As a new trader it can be difficult to find your footing, either when it comes to a specific business sector or even which market you are interested in trading in. While it is important that you fully explore your options, at the same time it is equally important that you find a specialty and give your learning some focus. Trying to master more than one type of trading at once is too monumental a task to ever be considered legitimately worthwhile. What's more, a majority of the markets offer up the same general returns which makes jumping around not only difficult but without any real merit as well. Find a type of trading that you enjoy and stick with it and your overall results will be stronger every time.

Don't read too much into beginner's luck: As a new trader, if you happen to be lucky enough to experience a winning trading streak early on it is important to not let it go to your head. While it may seem as though many of the suggestions outlined above don't apply to you, it will be important to try and retain perspective and understand that statistically speaking you are simply looking at a greater run of bad luck in the future. It is especially important to build a reliable trading foundation and skipping steps now will only lead to greater issues down the line.

Chapter 7:
Index Funds Versus Stocks

If you are interested in investing in stocks, this doesn't mean you are limited to traditional stock market trading practices, instead you can also choose a collection of index funds which are each made up of a collection of different stocks. One approach isn't unilaterally preferred to the other, however, as both have their own strengths and weaknesses which are outlined in detail below.

Traditional stocks

When you purchase individual shares of a given company's stock you are buying into that company for good or for ill. In exchange you will sometimes get dividends, and if the company in question stays profitable for an extended period of time then you will see positive appreciation as well. If you manage to get in during an early stock offering for a company that ultimately becomes a household name then you can likely retire, assuming you purchased enough shares to begin with. For example, if you invested in Walmart during their initial stock offering then a $10,000 investment would now be worth $10 million if you had reinvested the intervening earnings in additional stock as well. On the other hand, sometimes companies that seem extremely profitable from the outside simply implode. For example, if you had invested $10,000 in Enron during its initial public offering then that currently would be worth $0.

Index funds

Alternatively, you could invest in index funds wherein each fund is actually a number of stock based around a certain index, or sector of the market; common indexes include the Dow Jones and S&P 500. Essentially, if you are buying into an index fund you could be buying into anywhere from dozens to thousands of different stocks all at once. As such, you trade the risk and rewards of one major company for the lower risk and overall lower rewards of a greater number of smaller companies. Because at least 50 percent of the companies in question are likely to be profitable in a given year, investing in an index requires very little effort while still bringing in an average 5 to 7 percent yearly return on investment. What's more, instead of having to look over all of the financials, all you have to do is look over your portfolio every once and a while and ensure things are still going in the right direction.

Choosing an index fund

When it comes to choosing an index fund, the first thing you are going to want to consider are the same things you would consider when investing in traditional stocks, your accepted level of risk, the anticipated length of your investment and your overall goals when it comes to investing in both the short and the long term. With these answers in mind, you will then need to choose if you are more interested in an index fund that is mutual or exchange traded. If you aren't sure which is right for you, consider the following:

- If you are planning for the long term, then an IRA that is index mutual fund based is probably the best choice. You may be even able to find variations on this account in your area that are transaction free.

- If you are looking for something more active, then an exchange traded fund is probably a better choice because they can be traded in the same fashion as traditional stocks. You are more in control when it comes to both limits and entering a given trade while also having more variety as you are not limited to a single index.

With the general type of fund, you are looking for in mind, the next thing you are going to want to do is find one with the overall lowest expense ratio possible. Outside of that you are going to want to ensure that the fund you choose successfully tracks the index in question. This can be determined by checking their performance history in relation to the performance available of the index in question. First and foremost, you are going to want to ensure the index that you ultimately choose is one that is going to match what your investment objectives are at the moment. If you are looking for growth that is speculative then a small cap index is going to be the right choice. Finally, it is important to keep in mind that just because an index fund minimizes the overall risk that you are taking on, it doesn't negate it entirely and indexes can be just as volatile as the stock market as a whole.

Indexes to choose from

If you haven't yet done much research on a given sector of the market to yet believe that it is only going to improve, then sticking with the major indexes is a valid choice. These major indexes include:

The Dow Jones Industrial Average: The Dow Jones Industrial Average is the most well-known of all the indexes and currently tracks 30 major corporations. Because it only tracks a relatively small number of companies it often behaves differently than the market as a whole. The companies that the Dow takes into account include Apple, American Express, Boeing, Caterpillar, Cisco Systems, Chevron, Coca-Cola, DuPont, ExxonMobil, General Electric, Goldman Sachs, Home Depot, IBM, Intel, Johnson and Johnson, JPMorgan Chase, McDonald's, 3M Company, Merek, Microsoft, Nike, Pfizer, Procter & Gamble, The Travlers Company, UnitedHealth, United Technologies, Visa, Verizon, Walmart and Walt Disney.

S&P 500: The S&P 500 tracks a much broader range of US companies than the Dow Jones which means it is a more diversified look at the market as a whole. In general, the companies that are represented here are large and well established in their market of choice. If you invest in the S&P 500 then you are mitigating risk from any individual sector and are only really at risk to the whims of the market as a whole. If you are happy with the bare minimum return on your investment in an extremely reliable fashion, then this is for you.

Russell 2000: The Russell 2,000 Index is made up of 2,000 smaller US companies that are often still making a name for themselves. This index has a higher amount of risk in the short term though the overall profit margin in the long term tends to be greater as well as it is likely that at least a few of these companies will go on to major success over the course of a long term investment.

Qualities of a good index fund

While there is often less overall risk to many index funds, the shear fact that there are so many of them can make picking the right one for you harder than it might appear at first glance.

What follows are the types of ideal qualities you should hope to find in any index fund that you invest in.

Try and stay broad: What makes an index fund so appealing is that you have so many more opportunities for things to go right than with a single stock. As such, the best index funds capitalize on this broad strokes approach to diversify as much as possible. If you pick a fund that has an extremely narrow focus, then you could have likely bought into the same stocks instead for a smaller overall amount of fees. Keep it broad and protect your investments.

Know what you are investing in: This is another way to play to the strengths of index funds in general, keep the amount of research to a minimum and pick an index that contains a large number of companies that you are at least generally familiar with. If you are going to go to all of the work to research an obscure index fund, then you might as well take things another step further and do all of the research required to invest in stocks individually. Keep it simple and keep it broad for the most reliable results.

Stick to as few variables as possible: The greatest strength of index funds is in the way that the remove a number of variables from the investing conversation that most investors are never going to be able to affect, or even understand completely. Once again, the best indexes are the simplest ones with the fewest variables. The simpler that an investment is, the less there is that can cause it to fail, it is as simple as that.

Chapter 8:
Bears and Bulls

Before you head off into the world of stock market investment or trading, the terms bear market and bull market warrants a discussion all their own. This is because you are likely to run into them at nearly every turn and what they mean can be different depending on who is doing the classifying. These terms and their relevant classifications are going to play a major part in your investment success which is why it is so important that you can attribute them to a concrete definition. Essentially, the terms bear and bull are used to describe both how the market is currently doing and how traders and investors perceive that it is doing.

If the market is said to currently be in a bullish way, then this means that the market as a whole is on a positive trend which means share prices are going to increase consistently for a prolonged period. When the overall economy is strong and unemployment isn't growing then investors are more likely to have a bullish outlook on the market as well which means they believe that the current uptrend is going to continue. If, however, it is currently a bear market then that means that the market as a whole is doing poorly and share prices across the board are regularly dropping. If the economy is slowing and unemployment is rising, then investors and traders will have a bearish outlook as well.

How these terms came to represent market conditions is often considered a mixture of a few facets of life in the Elizabethan era. First of all, arena fights between bears and bulls were a common attraction in those days and when the two animals fought one another, the bear attacked used a downward slash and the bull attacked by attempting to gore upwards with its horns. The use of these terms in association with market movement then grew further as a market arose around bear skins during this same time. In this market, those who sold the bear skins typically sold off their stock before it had even been received. These folks were the original short sellers as they wanted overall prices to decrease so they could make a profit on the difference between what they had convinced others to pay and what they could then pay themselves. As this process started to apply to other markets as well the term bears spread to anyone hoping to make money on a down market.

Important characteristics to consider

While determining the current state of a market is relatively easy when it is in full swing one direction or the other, picking up on the signs of a coming bull or bear switch as early as possible is key to profiting from the change before everyone else has already gotten on board. The characteristics outlined below are many of the most common factors attributed to each market type, but it is important to keep in mind that you may or may not see each when a change to the market is on its way. Keep an eye out for all of them and you will never be surprised.

Demand versus supply: If the market is moving in a bullish direction then you will often see demand start to outpace supply. If you suddenly see prices starting to spike despite no new news and a period of low volatility, then you know that a bull market is to blame. The opposite is going to be the case if the market is moving into a bearish period and supply will exceed demand, naturally causing prices to begin to droop as a result.

Word on the street: It is important to always keep in mind that the way those who interact with the market feel about it is going to be just as important as the conditions the market is actually facing. As such, it pays to keep your ear to the ground when it comes to the scuttlebutt in the financial sector about the general state of things. If you hear that new companies are having an easy time finding investors or that market participation is climbing, then you know you are moving towards a market that is bullish. If, however, you discover that fixed-income securities are increasing in popularity, especially if market participation is dropping then you can have good idea that the market is going to turn the other direction sooner than later.

Overall activity in the economy: It is easy for many new traders to get so focused on the market itself that they forget that the companies that are being traded in the market are also making moves in the real world as well. If a number of prominent businesses report unexpected losses in a given quarter or consumer spending is down in general, then this is a good sign that the market is going to soon be moving towards a bearish state. On the other hand, if you see reports that consumer spending is on the rise, or likely to be on the rise soon, then you can expect the market to respond in kind by moving towards a bullish state as well.

Trends

When it comes to determining which direction the market is going to be moving in, you are going to want to consider the long term patterns and disregard everything else. If you focus on events in only the short term, then it will be much easier for you to mistake the market's natural haphazard reaction to a common event as proof of movement in one direction or another. Likewise, these smaller movements could simply be an unrelated trend in the short term or simply the market naturally correcting a previous disparity. Additionally, if you look at a long enough timeline you can see even broader changes to don't affect the type of trading that you are looking to do.

The difficulty in determining the exact timeframe for optimum viewing can be mitigated by considering the amount of change that has occurred in a series of expanding time frames. Specifically, if you take the time to look through multiple different indexes and note that a majority of them have moved in one direction or another by at least 15 percent. You can then expand your scope out until the trend is no longer apparent and then determine if the strength of the trend in question makes it seem likely that it is going to continue for a long enough period of time that you can actually make a profit off of it.

What's more, when looking for bear or bull trends it is important to keep in mind that the market can also be in neither a bull or a bear phase. This is referred to as market stagnation and it can happen when the market is temporarily struggling to find the right direction to move in. You will know a period of stagnation when you see it by the numerous different up and down movements that it creates as the market jumps back and forth before a dominant direction is chosen.

Taking advantage

In order to best take advantage of the oncoming change in market direction, you are going to want to take different actions for the two directions the market might move. If the market is moving towards a bullish phase, then you will want to buy into the trend as early as possible and then hold onto it until early signs start indicating the good times are coming to an end. It is important to not try and stay in for too long if you don't want to cut into those profits you are trying so very hard to keep. Finally, it is important to keep in mind that an oncoming bull market doesn't mean that you will experience no losses, it just means that the losses will be canceled out in the long run.

On the other hand, if the market is moving into a bear market then you are going to find a majority of the profit that can be made will come from short sales. You can also be on the lookout for the type of stocks that are not being effected by the current trend as they are likely resistant to the underlying cause. Finally, once you see signs of the bearish state start to ease, you can buy in with the expectation of short term losses in hopes of major gains.

Conclusion

Thank for making it through to the end of *Stock Trading: Definitive Beginner's Guide,* let's hope it was informative and able to provide you with all of the tools you need to achieve your goals both in the near term and for the months and years ahead. Remember, just because you've finished this book doesn't mean there is nothing left to learn on the topic. Becoming an expert at something is a marathon, not a sprint, slow and steady wins the race.

The next step is to stop reading already and to get started determining which type of stock market trading is best for you. Remember, regardless of which avenue you choose, it is important you don't get serious about it until after you have written up your own plan. Making the decision to trade without a plan is like jumping out of an airplane without a backup parachute, ensure you aren't in for a rough landing and plan before you start trading, you'll be glad you did.

Finally, if you found this book useful in anyway, a review on Amazon is always appreciated!

www.ingramcontent.com/pod-product-compliance
Lightning Source LLC
Chambersburg PA
CBHW070418190526

45169CB00003B/1313